MW01493605

FROM BUZZ TO BOND

HOW TO STOP CHASING HYPE & BUILD A LASTING MUSIC CAREER

HUNTER CAT PRESS / NEW YORK

Other Books By Ariel Hyatt

The Ultimate Guide to Music Publicity
Proven Strategies for Getting Featured in Blogs, Playlists &
Traditional Media

Crowdstart
The Ultimate Guide to a Powerful and Profitable Crowdfunding Campaign

Social Media Tuneup
Assess, Upgrade and Rock Your Entire Digital Presence

Cyber PR for Musicians:
Tools, Tricks & Tactics for Building Your Social Media House

Cyber PR for Musicians: Teachers Guide
Tools, Tricks & Tactics for Building Your Social Media House

Music Success In 9 Weeks
A Step-By-Step Guide on How to Use Social Media & Online Tactics

Musician's Roadmap to Facebook and Twitter
A Complete Guide to Getting Liked, Followed, and Heard

TABLE OF CONTENTS

DEDICATION

To Musicians Everywhere.
Without you, there would be no soundtrack to my life.

"
We are in a time where art matters more than ever. Connection matters more than ever. You need to make art as your outlet, and fans need it as their connection point and healing balm.

————————————————

Hello.

We are living in strange times. The world feels more fractured than ever—uncertainty is high, attention spans are short, and trust is hard to come by. For musicians, competition has never been fiercer. With over 120,000 tracks uploaded daily to streaming platforms, the sheer volume of music has turned visibility into an uphill battle.

Social media—once a place for community and connection—has become an **algorithm machine**, prioritizing viral moments over **meaningful relationships.** Artists are constantly told they need to "go viral" or rack up streaming numbers, but the reality is, **hype doesn't equal longevity**. The industry's latest obsession? **Superfans.**

For the foreseeable future, countless new platforms, services, and schemes will emerge—some helpful, many exploitative—all designed to extract money from fans. The competition for attention will only intensify, and independent artists who want real, sustainable careers must rethink their approach.

I have a front-row seat, watching artists pour money, time, and energy into marketing strategies that create nothing but dopamine hits and vanity metrics.

I call this **Buzz Marketing.**

Buzz Marketing makes numbers that look good from a distance, but it doesn't build real fans, true engagement, or sustainable income. The moment the ad budget dries up, so does the so-called success. This is not a career—it's a trap.

That's why I wrote From *Buzz to Bond.* I care deeply about musicians, and I'm tired of watching them struggle while missing the **bigger picture.**

This is where **Bond Marketing** comes in.

You won't have to execute all 10 steps of the funnel to create a more bonded fanbase, but you will have to shift your **mindset.**

That is what this little book aims to **do.**

The artists who build lasting careers aren't the ones who chase algorithms or trends.

They are the ones who create real connections, inspire loyalty, and cultivate a community that stands by them—not just for one release, but for a lifetime.

Your music deserves more than fleeting attention. It deserves a fanbase that truly cares.

This is your invitation to step off the hamster wheel of hype and build something real.

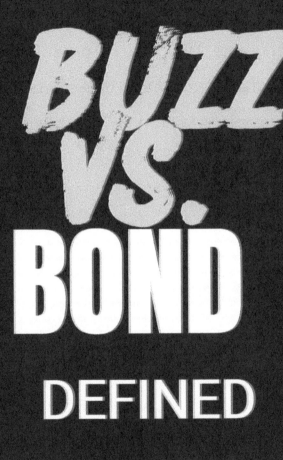

BUZZ VS. BOND

DEFINED

Buzz Marketing

The numbers game. The chase for playlists, viral moments, and passive streams that create the **illusion of success** but **fail to build lasting careers or create real fans.**

Bond Marketing

The real game. The strategies that **build direct connections, fandom,** and **authentic community—** where superfans are born, not through hype, but through time, consistency, and **meaningful engagement.**

If You Have No Fans, You Have No Superfans

Superfans aren't new. Musicians have always needed **deeply invested fans to survive since music was invented.**

In the digital realm, Kevin Kelly's *1,000 True Fans* theory laid this out in 2008 and contextualized the industry conversation. And yet, in 2024-5, we've seen a resurgence of this idea, as if it's some kind of *revelation*. It's not.

> ## Superfans aren't new. Musicians have always needed deeply invested fans to survive since music was invented.

Superfans Aren't The Starting Point - *Any* Fans Are.

Superfans are what happens over time with effort, consistent music, touchpoints, and strategy. Sadly, distractions have gotten in the way in recent years, and many musicians have stopped getting fans.

Meet My Client John Dough (Not His Name, Of Course)

John Has Created A Major Problem

John is an extraordinarily talented artist with serious financial backing. This has allowed him to invest heavily in Buzz Marketing—long-term Spotify playlisting campaigns that generate millions of plays and keep the algorithm working in his favor, social media managers crafting content and running ads to inflate his numbers, an expensive radio promoter, a national publicist, and even a European tour arranged through a hired strategist.

From the Outside, John's Career Looks Impressive

But behind the scenes, his manager (for hire) called me in desperation. Despite all the money invested, the million+ streams, and all the followers, not a single booking agent would take him on—because John can't fill even a small club or bar outside his hometown.

John is caught in the toxic cycle of Buzz Marketing. The moment his ad dollars stop, the streams drop, and engagement dries up.

When you peel back the layers of John's ad-driven strategy, you'll find that much of the "buzz" is bought in regions where clicks are cheap, building an audience in places irrelevant to his career. Booking agents see right through this, and the moment they check analytics or real-world demand, the illusion crumbles.

John is an extreme case because he has a big budget—but almost every musician I know has, at some point, invested in **Buzz Marketing**.

3 CORE PRINCIPLES OF BUZZ MARKETING

BE WIDELY DISCOVERABLE

Make your music and content easy to find – But mass visibility doesn't necessarily equal meaningful connection.

RIDE TRENDS

Leverage fads to catch algorithms and increase exposure – Chasing trends can make you feel disposable, forcing you to constantly adapt instead of building a lasting identity.

PAY TO MAXIMIZE REACH

Use ad platforms to build on Spotify and socials – Relying on paid reach can be a never-ending expense, with no guarantee of real fan loyalty or long-term impact.

10 EXAMPLES OF BUZZ MARKETING STRATEGIES

Riding Dumb Social Media Trends:
Posting TikToks, Instagram Reels, or YouTube Shorts with trending sounds or hashtags.

Influencer Collaborations:
Paying influencers or other artists to expand your reach without goals and context

Spotify Ad Studio:
We have never heard of a successful Spotify Ad campaign that really made a difference.

Guaranteed Playlist Submissions
Hiring companies that make guarantees about how many plays you will get or get you on weird playlists that are driven by ads

Radio Promotions:
College, specialty, or commercial terrestrial radio campaigns.

Growth Hacking:
Hiring apps and services that guarantee real followers (they never are)

Meta Ads:
Using Meta (Facebook/Instagram) to drive likes or plays with no secondary strategy

YouTube Promo:
Buying huge amounts of plays that rarely have comments or subscribers (and mostly will get you plays in countries you don't need fans in!)

PPC Ads:
Pay Per Click (yes, still like it's 1999!)

Traditional Ads:
I have seen multiple artists go crazy with this one, including some who paid for billboards in Times Square.

Why Buzz Marketing Proliferates

The False Perception *Feels* REAL

Buzz Marketing can make it feel like you're winning. Big numbers, viral moments, and algorithmic boosts make it seem like fans are flooding in. But without real engagement, those numbers can be deceiving. You might think you have an audience, but until they show up for you—at shows, in your inbox, or in your community—you don't actually know who they are or if they'll stick around.

Buzz Marketing Allows You to Hide

Real fan relationships require interaction, vulnerability, and effort. Buzz Marketing, on the other hand, lets you stay at arm's length. It feels easier—let the numbers do the talking, let the ads handle the reach—but this means you're missing out on true fan connection. Artists who lean only on Buzz often never develop the confidence to connect meaningfully with their audience.

Almost All Buzz Marketing is Purchasable

Many companies and services are available to execute Buzz Marketing strategies for a fee. Be wary when promises of guaranteed plays on Spotify or follower numbers on social are involved. If it sound too good to be true it likely is.

Buzz Marketing Allows You to "Just Make Music"

I hear this all the time—musicians call my agency, and they don't *want* to do all of the things that building an authentic audience requires. "I just want to make music—I don't want to deal with all the marketing." And that's understandable. The work of building an engaged, bonded fanbase takes skill, patience, and consistency. If your goal is to create for the love of it with no pressure to monetize, that's absolutely okay! But if you want music to be your career, hiding behind Buzz won't get you there.

You Need Secondary Strategies

Buzz Marketing on its own is a game of fleeting impressions—your numbers may go up, but without a deeper strategy, those fans will slip through your fingers just as quickly as they appeared. A **secondary strategy** is the crucial missing piece: the system that ensures that once someone discovers you, there's a clear and compelling path for them to **bond** with your music and become a real fan.

A secondary strategy is the crucial missing piece: the system that ensures once someone discovers you, there's a clear and compelling path for them to bond with your music and become a real fan.

This means **not** throwing money at ads before you have a tested and proven way to attract and convert bonded fans. Buying social media ads only makes sense **after** you've built a foundation—when you know how to engage your audience, when you have content that consistently resonates, and when you have a system in place to turn casual listeners into long-term supporters.

Without this, ads become a black hole where money goes in and vanity metrics come out, and this leads to **Buzz Marketing Danger Loops.**

BUZZ MKTG

DANGER LOOPS

Buzz Marketing Danger Loops

Something awful takes over in your overwhelm and desire for as many people as possible to hear your music. This can be fueled by looking at others' Spotify and social numbers or by bad advice you may have read about what really counts in today's landscape.

I like to call this awful thing a **Buzz Marketing Danger Loop**. These can be endless, like the proverbial dog chasing its tail, and they create another problem, which is they give you dopamine hits as they inflate your numbers, which can feel good; however,

You may have become addicted to the dopamine hits caused by **Buzz Marketing Danger Loops**, and this has warped your sense of true fandom.

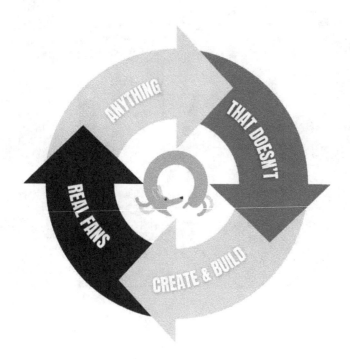

TikTok Doesn't Care If You Build An Audience

Following trends and sounds is usually not a way for potential fans to see and understand that you are a musician... You may get a viral moment on TikTok, but catching viral moments won't quickly or directly help you build a bonded fanbase.

Facebook & IG Also Don't Care

Zuck doesn't care about letting your followers on Facebook or Instagram see your posts. He also doesn't care about the mental health of teen girls or our collective civil society. That's not where he makes money. Facebook and Instagram make money by mining your personal information for data points. The more data points you share, the more data they have to target ads they sell. Facebook posted $160 billion in advertising revenue in 2024 and that's what they care about!

Short-Term ROI

When you spend ad dollars running Meta ads to drive streams on Spotify, you pay for *impressions*, not relationships. Even if your campaign is targeted—say, "Nashville-based indie folk listeners"—most clicks result in one-off streams. Without a direct way to capture that fan (email, social follow, etc.), they're likely gone after one listen.

The Repeat Touchpoint Problem

Spotify and TikTok give you limited data. You can't effectively retarget or even know who they are unless they take an extra step (like following you directly). This makes it hard to create the **repeated touchpoints** needed to cultivate superfans; I'll get to that later.

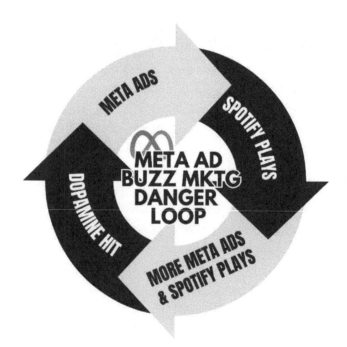

Why Cheap Ads Can Hurt Your Local Cred

Imagine you're an artist in Nashville trying to book gigs at local clubs. To get booked, you need to prove you have a local following—seems obvious, right?

But if you rely on cheap digital ads to boost your streams, you might end up attracting listeners in places like South America simply because the ad rates (CPM) are lower there. While this may inflate your streaming numbers, it doesn't help you build a real audience in Nashville—one that actually shows up to your gigs or buys your merch.

A local promoter isn't going to be fooled. A quick look at your Spotify analytics will reveal the truth: if most of your streams come from overseas, but you have little to no local traction, it raises red flags. Instead of looking like a serious contender for a gig, you risk appearing as an artist with inflated numbers but no real hometown support.

You Could Get Riddled With Bots or Banned From Spotify

Many playlisting services use pay-to-play tactics that result in bots or disengaged listeners. Even if streams go up, these may not be real fans interacting with you. Worse, Spotify's algorithm might deprioritize your track if it detects low engagement (like skips). Even worse, your Spotify account could get riddled with bots, and you will have a problem that is hard to undo. Then Spotify will punish you which may result in a strike against you.

Danger Loop IRL Scenario:

I know an artist who, after months of paying for Spotify Danger Loops, was left with a significant amount of streams in South America. Seduced by this data, he decided to record tracks in Spanish (he is not a Spanish speaker, which was not part of his brand) because he became convinced that his fan base was there. Then, he paid for more ads to promote the Spanish song, and you guessed it - created ANOTHER Buzz Marketing Danger Loop. See how these loops lead to warped perception and cause you to focus on the **wrong things?**

Your Dopamine Attachment Is Real

Danger Loops have created a vicious cycle. **Your Dopamine Attachment Is Real**: You might expect one viral moment to do the work of building a fanbase, but it won't, and this is why **Buzz Marketing** is deceiving. It will result in countless hours chasing trends and algorithms, hoping for a breakthrough. But streams and five-second scrolls don't translate into real fans. Instead, you will feel pressured to keep feeding the algorithm, burning time and energy to maintain appearances.

The biggest mistake artists make is assuming that awareness alone equals long-term success. But Buzz without Bond leads to a revolving door of passive engagement.

The biggest mistake artists make is assuming that awareness alone equals long-term success. But Buzz without Bond leads to a revolving door of passive engagement—followers who drift in and out, streams that vanish when the ad budget runs dry, and numbers that look great on paper but don't translate into real-world impact.

Please Play The Long Game

It may not feel as satisfying to connect with **one** person as it does to rack up **1,000 plays**, but over time, as you build real bonds, it becomes more manageable—and ultimately, more rewarding. Consistency and repetition in nurturing fan relationships create deeper engagement, which leads to a more sustainable career, not just fleeting numbers.

Okay, I'm Done Talking About How Ineffective Buzz Marketing Is.

If you want a real career and want to quit your day job or have visions around monetizing, then you must master *Bond Marketing.*

"

If you want a real career and want to quit your day job or have visions around monetizing, then you must master Bond Marketing.

Before We Move On... you may be thinking there's nothing wrong with Buzz Marketing and

Your definition of Success Might Stop at Buzz Marketing, (and That's *OKAY)*

Not every artist is destined for—or even suited for what it takes to build a bonded fanbase in today's climate.

"

The notion that *every* artist must achieve massive streaming and follower numbers to validate their art is part of the toxic, numbers-driven mindset perpetuated by platforms and industry that made Buzz Marketing so prevalent in the first place.

If creating Buzz Marketing numbers makes you feel happy, and satisfied, stop reading this right now and feel confident that you have done enough.

But I suspect you may be feeling empty, depleted, and depressed JUST *LIKE JOHN DOUGH.*

BOND MKTG

THE PATH TO REAL FANS

THE REST OF THIS BOOK IS GOING TO FOCUS ON BOND MARKETING

Bond Marketing represents actual fan creation strategies—tactics designed to foster loyalty and deepen relationships with fans. These strategies ensure that fans stay engaged and invested in the artist's journey.

 Bond Marketing represents actual fan creation strategies—tactics designed to foster loyalty and deepen relationships with fans. These strategies ensure fans stay engaged and invested in the artist's journey.

A Note About Tools & Platforms

This book will not be filled with platforms and tools to use; there are many, and I have my favorites. The point is to show you the philosophy and visually examine the bond marketing funnel. I do not want you to get tripped up on platforms, but rather, let this philosophy sink in. The tools are plentiful and easy to find.

I also have not included a large number of statistics and quotes about the state of the business as, again, that will overwhelm you (trust me, I lose sleep every night).

Let's focus on the task at hand, shall we?

3 CORE PRINCIPLES OF BOND MARKETING

BUILD OWNERSHIP

Instead of relying solely on social media algorithms, establish direct communication channels like email lists, memberships, and a personal website to maintain control over your audience and ensure long-term engagement.

FOSTER COMMUNITY

Encourage connection, create a sense of belonging, and build a culture where supporters feel like they are part of something special.

PROVIDE VALUE

Create offerings that deepen fan engagement and get you paid, but first, get vulnerable and honest.

10 EXAMPLES OF BOND MARKETING STRATEGIES

Being Vulnerable:
Sharing raw, unpolished moments of your creative process and rehearsals, or give life updates to bring fans deeper into your world.

Meaningful Interactions:
Connecting genuinely.

One-on-One Outreach:
Sending DMs, voice notes, or personalized video messages to engaged fans to make them feel seen and valued.

Live Shows:
You play, they attend; it's amazing

IRL Events:
Getting out into the world and hanging with fans.

VIP Experiences:
Offering exclusive in-person or virtual experiences.

Email List:
Build and maintain an email list to communicate directly with your fans.

Online Fan Groups:
Creating Fan Sanctuaries

Interactive Online Events:
Hosting Zooms, Livestreams, or Q&A sessions.

Juicy Offers:
Providing fans with unique items and music created only for them

The Challenges Ahead

This will take hard work.

This marketing style takes effort, and it's not easy to outsource because there is no one-size-fits-all solution. Bond Marketing requires a custom approach from each musician, and yeah, it will take effort.

Up Until Now, You Have Had Misplaced Priorities:

You may have done a lot of Buzz Marketing until now. It's time to shift your mindset from **numbers** to **nurture**.

You'll Have to Master New Systems:

Capturing fans requires organization—knowing where to direct them, how to keep them engaged, and having a clear "what's next" for every fan.

Vulnerability is Part of This Journey

You will be rebooting (or at the very least seriously tweaking) your marketing strategy, and to make it meaningful, you may feel vulnerable.

Reframing Bond Marketing As Mindset (An Inner Game)

At its core, marketing isn't just about tactics—it's about *mindset*. If you frame Bond Marketing as a chore, it will always feel like an uphill battle. But everything changes when you shift your perspective and view it as an opportunity to cultivate genuine relationships. Your fans aren't just numbers on platforms; they're humans who crave connection, inspiration, and belonging.

Approaching marketing with a mindset of **curiosity** and **generosity**—rather than pressure and expectation—will make it feel less like a burden and more like an extension of your creative expression. You build something that lasts when you commit to consistent, meaningful engagement. Marketing is about making potential fans *feel* something and keeping them in your world long after the song ends.

Instead of bonding as "work," you must consider it a creative journey to building relationships. Fans want to connect with artists, and small, consistent actions can lead to significant results over time. **One fan at a time will be the way this battle gets won.**

BOND MKTG
YOUR THREE COMMUNITIES

CYBER PR

YOUR 3 COMMUNITIES

♥ SUPERFANS

BONDED TRUE FANS
5+ TOUCHPONTS

JOINED FAN SANCTUARY OR EMAIL LIST
ATTEND STREAMS & SHOWS OFTEN
FOLLOWING CLOSELY ON SOCIALS
SPREAD THE WORD
FREQUENT BUYERS

★ ENGAGED FANS

ACTIVE ONLINE AUDIENCE
2-5 TOUCHPOINTS

ENGAGE SOMETIMES ON SOCIALS
FOLLOW ON MORE THAN 1 SOCIAL
LIGHT STREAMING OF MUSIC
OPEN SOME EMAILS
RESPOND TO CTAS

((•)) AMBIENT FANS

PASSIVE ONLINE AUDIENCE
0-2 TOUCHPOINTS

AWARE OF YOU, DON'T YET INTERACT
MAY NOT HAVE HEARD MUSIC (YET!)
COULD BE A HASHTAG FOLLOWER
SAW AN AD AND TOOK NOTICE
FOLLOW BECAUSE OF YOUR CAT, FOOD, ETC.

Your 3 Communities:
A Framework for Building Relationships

Every artist has three communities, which are separate from one another.

The challenge most artists face isn't just *reaching* fans—it's understanding that **not all fans are the same**. Yet, many artists make the mistake of using a *one-size-fits-all* approach when embarking on Bond Marketing, treating every follower and listener like they have the same level of investment.

Being online has made fan connection easier *and* way more complicated at the same time. While we have unlimited access to billions of people, so does everyone else, making it critical to have a system in place because it's more challenging than ever to stand out. In the rush to reach as many people as possible, many artists overlook a crucial reality: not everyone engaging with you is equally invested in your journey and will come along.

Some may have followed you because they liked your sunglasses or cat, unaware you even *make* music. Others interact frequently; **these are the fans you will start gathering first.**

Understanding these differences—and crafting distinct communication strategies for each group—is the key to building lasting, meaningful relationships with your fans. It's not just about *growing* your audience; it's about nurturing the right connections in practical ways.

SUPERFANS
BONDED TRUE FANS
5+ TOUCHPONTS

JOINED FAN SANCTUARY OR EMAIL LIST
ATTEND STREAMS & SHOWS OFTEN
FOLLOWING CLOSELY ON SOCIALS
SPREAD THE WORD
FREQUENT BUYERS

Community #1: Superfans
5+ Touchpoints

These are fans to whom you are most deeply bonded. Superfans are defined as engaging with an artist in five or more ways, according to research by Luminate. According to their 2023 Mid-Year Music Report, superfans are quantified as fans interacting with an artist across multiple touchpoints—including streaming, attending shows, purchasing merch, engaging on social media, or subscribing to platforms. This aligns with their finding that superfans spend significantly more money on music (up to 80% more monthly) than the average music listener.

This is why gathering them where you can see and communicate with them is essential - they are your lifeblood. Superfans are also the ones most likely to share your music with others—so making them feel valued isn't just about deepening their connection; it's about expanding your reach organically.

ENGAGED FANS
ACTIVE ONLINE AUDIENCE
2-5 TOUCHPOINTS

ENGAGE SOMETIMES ON SOCIALS
FOLLOW ON MORE THAN 1 SOCIAL
LIGHT STREAMING OF MUSIC
OPEN SOME EMAILS
RESPOND TO CTAS

Community #2: Engaged Fans
2-5 Touchpoints

Your *Engaged Fans* bridge your Ambient Fans and your Superfans. They like your posts, comment occasionally, and open some of your emails. While they may not yet buy merch or come to every show, they pay attention. This group has immense potential because they're already tuned in; they must be invited to come deeper into your world.

The key to nurturing Engaged Fans is *consistency and attention.* Respond to their comments, invite them into conversations, and create moments where they feel seen and appreciated. These fans are primed for deeper engagement—whether signing up for exclusive content, joining a private fan group, or making their first purchase. The more you give them reasons to stay connected, the more likely they will step into your inner circle of Superfans.

((•)) AMBIENT FANS
PASSIVE ONLINE AUDIENCE
0-2 TOUCHPOINTS
AWARE OF YOU, DON'T YET INTERACT
MAY NOT HAVE HEARD MUSIC (YET!)
COULD BE A HASHTAG FOLLOWER
SAW AN AD AND TOOK NOTICE
FOLLOW BECAUSE OF YOUR CAT, FOOD, ETC.

Community #3: Ambient Fans
1-2 Touchpoints

These fans are your Passive Online Audience, and they are your social media followers or people you reach with boosted posts or ads who are aware of you but don't actively communicate with you and may not have ever even heard your music (yet).

How to Consider These Communities Moving Ahead

Maintaining your relationship with these communities requires a different strategy because you have varying degrees of engagement with each.

How you create and develop your relationship with them should also be carefully considered. Yes, they will overlap, but not as much as you think.

From Understanding Your Communities to Creating Lasting Bonds

Recognizing that your audience exists in three distinct communities is the first step—but knowing how to move fans through these stages is where the magic of Bond Marketing happens.

To move fans through the three communities, you need a system that nurtures and deepens those relationships over time.

That's exactly what the **Bond Marketing Funnel** is designed to do.

Let's break it down step by step.

BOND
MKTG
FUNNELL

CYBER PR
BOND MARKETING FUNNEL

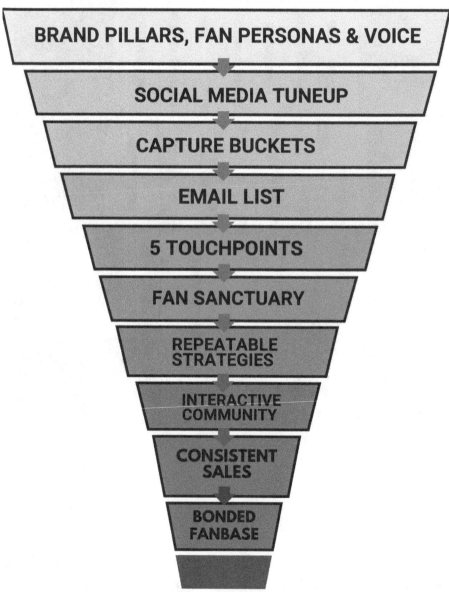

BRAND PILLARS, FAN PERSONAS & VOICE

SOCIAL MEDIA TUNEUP

CAPTURE BUCKETS

EMAIL LIST

5 TOUCHPOINTS

FAN SANCTUARY

REPEATABLE STRATEGIES

INTERACTIVE COMMUNITY

CONSISTENT SALES

BONDED FANBASE

The Bond Marketing Funnel

The funnel has ten parts. Start at the top and work your way through, building out each section as you move down the funnel. Of course, you release music and play live all the while.

Brand Pillars, Fan Personas & Voice

These elements need to be thought out and modified so that fans will easily recognize and be attracted to you.

Social Media Tuneup

Requires that you look around everywhere you are findable online and be sure that it is clear that you are a musician and that there are individual fan journeys set up on each platform.

Capture Buckets

The most critical part of the funnel, and countless artists skip over - you must create audience ownership and not give your power of Zuck, Eck or Google.

Email List

100% non-negotiable. You will need a robust list management system that you are adept at using.

Five Touchpoints

Most fans won't be instantly jumping into your buckets (I wish it were that easy) You need to touch them 5 times or more before you get buy-in.

The Bond Marketing Funnel

The funnel has ten parts. Start at the top and work your way through, building out each section as you move down the funnel. Of course, you release music and play live all the while.

Fan Sanctuary

Your dedicated fan space. By dedicated, I mean the whole world can't see what's happening there, and fans must opt-in to participate.

Repeatable Strategies

Once you have a feel for what works after you have tested quite a few ideas and options, you want to make sure whatever works is repeatable and semi- automated.

Interactive Fan Community

You have worked to gather them all together, and now it's time to bond. Best of all, everyone will see your messages and intentions every time.

Consistent Flow Of Sales

Ask fans to buy all kinds of things. And see your money come in.

A Bonded Fanbase

This is the end goal —a true community that supports and sustains you however you define this.

BRAND PILLARS, FAN PERSONAS & VOICE

Brand Pillars, Fan Personas & Voice

Defining your brand pillars, fan personas, and messaging strategy is essential for building a strong, recognizable presence. Brand pillars shape your identity, fan personas clarify who you speak to, and your social media themes and voice ensure consistency across platforms. These elements create a cohesive brand that resonates with your audience and strengthens your connection with fans.

Brand Pillars

A brand pillar is a concise description that defines a core aspect of your identity, purpose, and values. Each pillar should capture "Who?" in a few words, highlighting a key characteristic of your musical essence and its significance to your artistry.

Clearly defined brand pillars help articulate your identity and audience, ensuring consistency across your website, social media, visuals, bio, and beyond. This cohesion strengthens your brand and deepens your connection with fans.

You should have between 3-5 Brand Pillars

Fan Personas

A fan persona represents the key traits of your most dedicated listener, answering, "Who is my ideal fan?" in just a few sentences. Defining these personas helps you better understand your audience, making it easier to create content, products, and experiences that resonate.

By identifying your fan personas, you can strategically target potential listeners, including those in other artists' communities who may connect with your music. Keeping your ideal fan in mind across all platforms will naturally attract more of them.

Engaging with other artists, industry peers, and musicians should be included, as it is necessary for building a strong, active fan base.

You should have between 3-5 Fan Personas.

Voice & Your Social Media Themes

To maintain a consistent brand voice, choose a tone that aligns with your personality and resonates with your ideal fans. Whether warm and conversational, bold and direct, or witty, your tone should feel authentic to you and remain uniform across posts, captions, and interactions. This consistency helps establish trust, recognition, and a deeper connection with your audience.

Social Media Themes are designed to help you streamline your content and stay focused when on socials. Aligned with your brand pillars and fan personas, they reinforce your identity and provide direction for what to post. Themes are a guide; they're not meant to limit you. Using them consistently while staying on track will strengthen your brand voice and create a more cohesive online presence.

Your primary theme should always be music—your artistry, creative process, performances, inspirations, and releases. Keeping music at the core ensures you attract and engage the right audience.

You should have between 3-5 Social Media Themes.

Social Media Tune Up

You need to review every platform and ensure you have set everything up to ensure your fan journeys are consistent and intriguing, as well as set out your buckets. This also includes your website.

As you move through each platform, be sure they are consistent, easy to navigate, and inviting fans to come along to the next touchpoint.

Do you have multiple intriguing CTAS that lead potential fans to an additional touchpoint?

I wrote a book that systematically walks you through your website and every social platform with easy-to-follow checklists on how to maximize and set up your fan journeys more effectively.

It covers the same process I use with my clients at Cyber PR to assess what needs to be optimized. It's designed to maximize and clarify your social media presence, increase the effectiveness of your website once a fan lands on it, and ultimately drive more fans towards your touchpoints

Buy it here: https://bit.ly/SMtuneup

A fan's journey starts when a fan or potential fan finds out about you. It's the journey they go on to discover you and what helps them become engaged fans.

Analyze Your Fan Journeys: They May Suck, So Fix Them Now

This fan journey could start on Google, Spotify, SoundCloud, or Instagram.

The word journey implies it won't end there – the potential fan will look in multiple places.

The fan journey will most likely start from their phone or computer or because they saw you live.

The key to creating solid fan journeys is analyzing yours online. What exactly happens during each one?

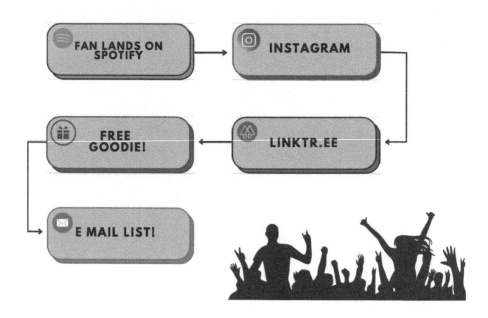

CYBER🅿🆁 FAN JOURNEY

Here's an Example of a Fan Journey That Starts at Spotify

A potential fan hears you on Spotify. They like what they hear, so click on your artist profile. Is that profile fully updated with the maximum amount of photos, an annotated bio, and links? Have you selected your focus track? Do you have links to your socials on your Spotify Profile? If not, your Fan Journey just ended!

But let's say you've done this well, and the fan heads to Instagram to continue their fan journey...

Now They're on Your Instagram

A fan heads to your IG. They click through to your profile. Is your bio clear, making it evident that you are the same musician they just saw on Spotify? Are the Profile images matching? Is the most recent release pinned to the top? Is there an updated short link in your bio? Have you made it clear throughout your posts that you have an active email list or a fan community? Do you respond when fans comment and seek connection? If not, that fan's journey may end.

They Love What They See, and They Click on Your Shortlink

They followed the link in your IG bio and are on your Linktr.ee! At the very top, you offer an exclusive track or a behind-the-scenes video that they can view only if they sign up for your email list.

You have just WON at building a compelling Fan Journey, and a new fan is onboard!

CAPTURE BUCKETS

 If it was pouring and you desperately needed water, would you put out just one bucket? Hell no, you would put out as many receptacles as you have available, right?

Therefore, there must be multiple places to gather fans.

Capture Buckets Include

Email List - This is the first one and nonnegotiable - Set up an email list properly using an actual email management program so you can parse, track, and set up autoresponders

Sanctuary - This is where superfans can join you in a closed ecosystem away from public open consumption. It can be as simple as a WhatsApp group, or you can use an app that manages this for you - there are many out there.

Exclusive Offers - Give something exclusive that can't be procured anywhere else like a free exclusive download, behind-the-scenes video, or song preview. They collect emails for you.

Shortlinks - Added to all social accounts that are easy to post on socials and share in emails.

Welcome Series - A written series of emails that fire out automatically after Email sign-up to create additional touchpoints.

CTA Social Posts - These invite actions - like "Join My Mailing List" or DM Me with one word for a sneak listen to an unreleased track. Videos can be compelling tools to drive actions.

Pre-Save Platforms that Gather Email Addresses - If you run pre-save campaigns, collect email addresses from fans who took the time to pre-save.

QR Codes - At shows and on marketing materials leading to free goodies/email lists or directly to fans via DM.

Text Message List- If you have a fanbase that will resonate, build a text messaging list with a short code opt-in.

 # EMAIL LIST

Email List

If you're serious about building a lasting music career, your email list is not optional—it's essential. Unlike social media, where algorithms dictate who sees your content, email gives you direct access to your fans on your terms.

A proper email list manager is crucial. If you don't yet understand email marketing fundamentals, now is the time to learn. Study autoresponder series, including welcome sequences (to onboard new fans) and sales sequences (to drive conversions).

> **"Email remains a significantly more effective way to acquire customers than social media–nearly 40 times that of [Social Media]**
>
> **– McKinsey & Company**

Why Musicians Resist Email Marketing

Over the years, I've heard two major excuses from artists who avoid email marketing:

Excuse #1: *"I don't want to bother my fans."*
Reality: Your real fans want to hear from you. The right emails feel like conversations, not sales pitches.

Excuse #2: *"I have nothing to say."* (translates to I do not have a show coming up)
Reality: You're already a storyteller—your music, journey, and creative process are full of stories worth sharing. The issue isn't that you have nothing to say; it's that you haven't yet found a way to communicate in a natural way **in email format.**

Please Stop Calling It a "Newsletter"

Words matter. The term "newsletter" alone can reduce open rates significantly. Most artists still treat email as a monthly recap or send emails only when they have a new release or show to promote.

From now on, ditch the "newsletter" mindset and consider your emails as serious invitations for fans to get to know you and enter your world.

How to Make Your Emails Better

Keep Them Simple: One topic per email. One clear CTA (Call To Action). Email marketing studies show that 200 words or 20 lines of text are effective lengths and then lead your readers to a longer post or to your site (this is where the Call To Action comes in)

Be Personal: Share behind-the-scenes moments, thoughts on your music, stories from the road, highlights from the season or try a deep personal story.

Be Consistent: Email at least once a month—ideally twice a month—to stay connected.

Track Results: It's essential to track your open rates and notice who responds to your emails. Answer everyone who takes the time to reply and encourage two-way interactions. This is where you get to know your fans, and shouting one way at them is not the way to bond.

5 TOUCHPOINTS

Five Touchpoints

To become bonded, each fan needs five critical touchpoints. This funnel part is labor-intensive: Building deeper connections takes time, energy, and focus.

This is where the Three Communities framework comes into play—you're guiding fans from Ambient to Engaged to Superfans (Bonded).

 Ambient Fans need consistent, meaningful interactions to move deeper into your world. The key is to create moments that feel personal and participatory.

Authenticity Turns Ambient Fans into Engaged Fans

Ambient Fans need consistent, meaningful interactions to move deeper into your world. The key is to create moments that feel personal and participatory. To do this, you must start with being open and willing to get vulnerable. No fans will be attracted to generic posts. For this, you need authenticity.

Authenticity means sharing something meaningful, personal, or inspiring that triggers an actual response from fans. If it moves you, it will likely move them. This is not about baring your soul or oversharing in a way that harms you, but you must be open to sharing something that resonates with you. Look back at your Brand Pillars here - is there something there that touched on this? If not, you may need to adjust.

9 Examples of Touchpoints

1. Authentic Social Media Interactions

Beyond the standard "thanks!" or generic emoji replies. Engage with fans personally—ask a follow-up question, crack a joke, or acknowledge something specific in their comment. The more authentic you are, the stronger the bond. Fans can tell when you're phoning it in versus genuinely engaging.

2. Zoom Hangouts & Virtual Meetups

Host casual Q&A sessions, acoustic performances, or behind-the-scenes storytelling events where fans can interact with you—and each other. These virtual gatherings make fans feel like they are part of an exclusive club, deepening their connection to you and your community.

3. Personalized Messages

When a fan consistently comments on your posts or shares your music, take the extra step to DM them a quick thank-you or start a short conversation. Showing appreciation can turn a casual fan into an engaged one.

4. In-Person Connection at Shows

Live performances are the ultimate bonding experience, but what happens after the show matters just as much. Spend time at the merch table and ensure every fan who wants to connect gets a moment with you. These face-to-face moments leave a lasting impression.

5. Cross-Platform Livestreams

Don't limit yourself to one platform. Stream simultaneously across social media and note the fans who show up regularly. Shouting them out by name, speaking to them during the streams, or remembering details about them can turn a passive viewer into a deeply engaged supporter.

9 Examples of Touchpoints

6. Charity Tie-Ins:

If you're passionate about a cause, invite your fans to participate in it. Whether it's a fundraiser, a benefit concert, or a merch collab with proceeds going to a good cause, giving fans a shared mission strengthens their emotional connection to you and your work.

7. Fan Shoutouts

Highlight top fans in your posts, videos, or livestreams. Whether reposting something they shared with a tag or calling them out by name and showing appreciation, these moments make your audience feel valued and encourage deeper engagement.

8. Polls and Q&As:

Give fans a voice in your creative process. Let them vote on setlists, merch designs, or upcoming content ideas. This will increase engagement and make fans feel part of your journey.

9. Community Engagement

Participate in relevant online spaces, such as Reddit threads, Facebook Groups, and Discord communities, where people already discuss your genre.

Each of these touchpoints isn't just a strategy—it's an opportunity to form meaningful, long-term connections. The more personal and intentional you are, the stronger the bond between you and your audience will become.

> **Each of these touchpoints isn't just a strategy—it's an opportunity to form meaningful, long-term connections. The more personal and intentional you are, the stronger the bond between you and your audience will become.**

Once you've engaged with a fan through 2-3 touchpoints, you will know:

- Their name
- What they like about you and why they interact
- What type of content or conversations they respond to

Moving From Engaged to Superfans (Bonded)

Look at the list of 9 above.
Once a fan is actively engaging, inviting them to take action is key.

Fans Need Educations

Fans may not be as smart as you think. They may not even realize how valuable an email sign-up is to you. I have a client who asked his followers across all social media how much money they thought he earned on Spotify (it was less than $250 a year). They all guessed $2,000 and up! Fans really don't understand. It is your job to educate them.

Fans Need Invitations

So, taking the initiative to **ASK** will go far! This means stopping trying to be elusive, confusing, cute, or coy and making a direct request. Your fans will see this as a personal invitation.

❝❝ **Stop trying to be elusive, confusing, cute, or coy, and directly make a request. Your fans will see this as a personal invitation to help you, and we all love to help one another.**

At this point, you'll have two types of Bonded Fans:

1. Fans who opted into your email list (direct connection).
2. Fans who join your sanctuary (interactive connection).

The Ideal Fans Will Do BOTH!

The more intentional and personal your approach, the more likely your fans will stick around not just for one release but for a lifetime.

6 FAN SANCTUARY

Your Fan Sanctuary: Where Superfans Thrive

Your fans deserve a place to connect with you and each other more deeply.

Think of your sanctuary as your *Inner Circle*, a space where true community can flourish.

"

Your superfans deserve a place to connect with you and each other more deeply. Think of this as your *Inner Circle*, a space where true community can flourish.

This dedicated, artist-driven environment offers exclusivity, meaningful engagement, and a **sense of belonging**. These *fan sanctuaries* create a safe space for you and those who care most about your music.

Here, you can offer exclusive content, host intimate live sessions, and make superfans feel valued—without fighting for visibility.

This is where you build something lasting.

Some Ideas to Keep Your Superfans / Bonded Fans Engaged

The more appreciated they feel, the more likely they will continue supporting your music, sharing it with others, and staying invested in your journey.

Create Real Talk – Build deeper relationships by having genuine conversations about things that matter to you and your fans. Whether sharing personal struggles, discussing causes, or opening up about the realities of being an independent artist.

Private Livestreams – Host members-only livestreams. Whether it's an intimate acoustic set, a deep dive into your songwriting process, or an informal hangout, making these experiences exclusive adds value.

Zoom Hangs & Q&As – Where fans can ask you questions, share their experiences, or just vibe with each other. Whether it's a structured Q&A, a listening party, or an unfiltered chat.

Community Input – Ask them to vote on setlists and merch designs or help choose your next cover song. When fans feel like their voices matter, they become insiders.

Shine A Light – Are your fans also creators? Celebrate their talent by featuring their artwork, music, covers, dance videos, recipes, etc.

Fan-Curated Playlists – Involve them in the music discovery process by inviting them to create and share playlists featuring your songs.

Community Challenges – Make engaging with your music fun and interactive. Run challenges like "Share a video using this song," "Create your cover art for my next single," or "Post your favorite lyric from my latest release." Add incentives like exclusive merch, signed memorabilia, or a private video message from you.

Exclusive Content – Share behind-the-scenes footage, unreleased tracks, personal stories, or sneak peeks of upcoming projects.

Giveaways & Special Rewards – Unique perks. These personalized incentives like early access to tickets, surprise merch drops, handwritten notes, or one-on-one virtual meet-and-greets.

The Most Effective of All: IRL Fan Meetups

You don't have to have a show to see your fans! Organize in-person meetups in your community. Invite fans to go bowling, play pool, have a beer, take a jog, do yoga, or sample tea. Take a walk in a museum, around town, or in a local park.

Be with people. Play music. Share ideas. Look at art.

Get inspired together.

If and when you travel, do the same in other places.

Try a Tourcation

Turn Travel Into Fan-Building Experiences

One of my Cyber PR team members takes a unique approach to touring—she calls it a "Tourcation." Instead of waiting for booking opportunities, she picks destinations she genuinely wants to visit and builds a show or VIP experience around them.

It all starts in real life—she connects with her fanbase in these cities, collaborates with fellow musicians, and organizes events that feel personal and special. Over time, the fans she meets become part of her sanctuary—her tight-knit community—acting as her personal talent promoters, helping her grow her audience in cities worldwide.

Building and maintaining a fan sanctuary isn't just about selling—it's about fostering **genuine relationships with lifelong supporters.**

REPEATABLE STRATEGIES

Repeatable Strategies

There will be some testing to see what works, and there won't be a one-size-fits-all approach, but in time, you will begin to see patterns emerge, and you will be able to create repeatable strategies that will work. My advice here is to focus on the ones that bring you joy. Joy creates ease, and ease will create consistency.

After you get the hang of it, the idea is that fans will invite others to join, and what you offer will be enticing and visible enough that more and more fans will come your way.

Go Slow

Focus on one platform and one core group of fans at a time before trying to do it all. A small, engaged base can become a bigger one naturally. This means picking ONE Fan Persona first and creating posts and messaging for them. This will help keep you focused.

Once you've built a **strong foundation** with your first fan persona and have a **repeatable system in place**, then—and only then—should you start expanding your reach. Focus on deepening engagement with your initial group before targeting the next.

Celebrate The Wins

Even one new email subscriber or personal fan message is a win. It's about progress, so take the time to acknowledge that you did this and let your fans know how much it means. Everyone loves an artist in gratitude.

Iterate Based on Feedback

Pay close attention to **what's working and what's not.** Which posts spark real conversations? Which offers drive the most signups? Which engagement tactics lead to genuine fan connections instead of passive likes?

Refine, tweak, and double down on what gets results. Let fan behavior guide your next steps—your audience will show you what they love if you listen.

By taking this approach, each new fan persona group you target will already have a tested, effective strategy behind it, making growth smoother and more impactful.

A Goal To Start - Make One Fan Per Day

Try setting this *micro-goal* of capturing just one new fan per day. If that feels like too much, go for one per week.

Over a year, that's a LOT of real connections
If you are looking for that key 1,000 true bonded fans, you have just gotten that much closer.

Once You Have An Organic System, Introduce Ad Spending

Ads can be a potent tool—but only when used at the **right time**. Before spending money on ads, ensure you have a proven system that organically attracts and bonds fans.

 If you are not engaging or converting people into true fans, no amount of ad dollars will fix that. Instead, ads should be used to amplify what's already working.

Here's When Investing in Ads Makes Sense

✓ You've identified a fan persona that responds well to your messaging.

✓ You have organic engagement—people commenting, sharing, and DMing.

✓ You've tested offers (like pre-saves, merch, or exclusive content) and know what resonates.

✓ You've built an onboarding system (such as an email welcome sequence or community group) that turns casual listeners into bonded fans.

When ads are used strategically to accelerate an already successful process, they can become a powerful tool to reach more of the right people—without wasting money on passive likes or fleeting attention.

Capture The Fun & Share

Do you know what all this goodwill and time together will foster? FOMO from those who have not yet joined your inner circle! Create videos where you have a blast with your fans, show off what you are creating, and post them on social media.

Interactive Community

Once they are in your Sanctuary, something else magical will unfold; your fans will start interacting and bonding with each other.

Building Fan-to-Fan Connections

This is where your role as a **matchmaker** comes in—creating spaces and moments that allow fans to bond over their love for the music.

Be a Great Host/Leader to Your Fans:

Name Your Sanctuary Or Fanbase

Give them an identity. Some examples: Dave Matthews has The Warehouse, Pearl Jam has the Ten Club, Aurora's supporters are known as Warriors & Weirdos, Doechii has her Swamp, Baby Tate has her Tater Tots, and of course, there's Lady Gaga's Little Monsters. Examples go on and on like this, and you should look at how artists you admire refer to and gather their fans. You might be inspired to come up with a name for your community.

Facilitate In-Person Connection Without You!

Choose an active member of your community to encourage meetups at shows or host pre/post-show gatherings. If you don't play live, have them host a picnic or do an activity that gets them together.

Empower Fan Ambassadors

Identify your most engaged fans and give them roles like moderating or hosting events you may not even attend! Then, recognize them publicly (with shoutouts in posts, thank-you notes, or exclusive perks.)

The Ripple Effect

When fans feel connected to each other, the community becomes self-sustaining—bringing new people into the fold.

The **fan-to-fan connections** build a community that grows and sustains itself, taking some of the burden off you.

Consistent Sales

Now we are finally at the part of the funnel that way too many artists want on day one. As you can see, you cannot get a consistent flow of sales until you have a consistent fanbase, a system for communicating with them, and a sense of what they want and what motivates them to buy.

Monetization should feel natural and exciting, unlike a sales pitch. Your bonded fans WANT to support you—you need to give them the right opportunities to do so. This makes the sales flow feel like a direct result of the fan-building process rather than a separate or forced step.

Involving fans in the process creates demand before launching anything, making fans feel invested in your offering.

So, before you rush to set up a merch store or start pushing sales, it's wise to ask your fans and community what they might want.

Ask First

A simple poll to your email list and posted in your sanctuary can help you discover

- **Type of Merch or Offerings** - What kinds of merch or experiences they'd be excited to buy
- **Pricing** - What price points feel right
- **High Tier Offerings** - What exclusive offers or perks would make them feel valued

Also, by doing this, you may discover some things you never would have thought of that could become income streams.

What to Sell

Here's how you can start generating consistent revenue:

Limited Drops – Instead of launching a vast merch store, start with limited-edition or signed items that create urgency and exclusivity. Pre-orders can help gauge interest before ordering stock.

Digital Collectibles & Personalized Content – Offer unique, low-cost, high-value digital items like handwritten lyric sheets, behind-the-scenes videos, or custom voice notes. These are easy to create and can be highly profitable.

Exclusive Live Access – Offer VIP meet-and-greet passes, soundcheck access, or private virtual concerts for fans who want a more intimate experience.

How to Sell

Make Offers Feel Like Events – Announce sales with a lead-up, behind-the-scenes content, or an exclusive reveal.

Use Email & Posts Strategically – Warm up fans by sharing the story behind the merchandise, song, or experience before asking them to buy.

Celebrate Buyers – Shout out fans who support you along the way.

Crowdfunding

If a continuous stream of selling things isn't your bag, know that you'll have a community ready to help if crowdfunding is how you want to leverage your fan base.

A crowdfunding campaign will be much easier to launch with an engaged email list and a fan sanctuary ready. Initial pledges will originate here.

Bonded Fanbase

This is in the final position of the funnel as it is the ultimate endpoint. A joyful, bonded fanbase will be there to **lift you up and support you for the long haul.**

A bonded fanbase is the foundation for a long, fulfilling career.

How Do You Know If You've Built a Bonded Fanbase?

It's not just about numbers. It's about **actions.**

A Bonded Fanbase is When:

• **Fans show up.** Not just online, also at your IRL meetups, at shows, in your livestreams, and in your sanctuary.

• **Fans engage.** They reply to your emails, comment on your posts, and share your music unprompted.

• **Fans buy.** They purchase merch, fund your projects, or support you through Patreon, Bandcamp, or memberships.

• **Fans advocate.** They introduce your music to others, bring friends to shows, and champion your work because it means something to them.

• **Fans stick around.** Even between releases, when you're not "active," they're still connected to your journey.

A Bonded Fanbase Is The Goal

Not fleeting viral moments, not streams that disappear when the playlist campaign ends—but fans who **choose to stay** because your music, presence, and story matter to them.

Ebbs and Flows

I understand that this funnel is a process, and I have oversimplified it to make it philosophical and digestible for you. Work and dedication will go into this and this process **ebbs and flows.**

I myself have been building up a community for decades, and some years, I have my foot on the gas, and some years, I don't - life happens to us, and there are times when our attention can't be on building, and it goes elsewhere.

This is unsustainable to do at 100% in perpetuity.

Many artists just activate one or two parts of the Bond Marketing funnel and they experience profound shifts.

Many artists just activate one or two parts of the Bond Marketing Funnel, and they experience profound shifts.

The Bond Marketing Mindset
Not Every Artist is Destined for This Whole Process

Some create music because it's their **passion, therapy, or self-expression.** You can make and release music as a creative outlet and still happily keep your day job, but that doesn't mean you are not a successful musician.

Some musicians have the drive, energy, time, and financial resources to turn music into a full-time business, but as I hope you have learned by reading this, it requires strategy, stamina, and sacrifices, not everyone is willing (or able) to make.

For artists who work slower, have niche audiences, or struggle with the constant pressure to constantly connect, this system may not be the right fit. Your music is still meaningful and impactful, and you should still create your music for the love of it and because you want to. Success can mean creating music that connects with an intimate circle of people.

For the past 20 years, one of my clients has held a full-time job, and now he has a family. He continues to release one great album every few years, plays a few meaningful gigs around his releases, and has a close community of fans who love and support him whenever he decides to reinvigorate his music life. When he has time and energy, he leans on Bond Marketing to re-inspire momentum.

You Can Use This Any Way That Works For You

I hope you have found this enlightening no matter where you are on your journey. It should inspire you to bond with more fans and provide clarity about the next steps to take, whatever they may be.

BOND MKTG

ACTION PLAN

The Bond Marketing Action Plan

☐ ## Look at Your Brand Pillars & Fan Personas
Are they clear to you? If not, create some that resonate with who you are today.

☐ ## Make Sure You Have a Voice
Look at your current posts, read your bio, and analyze how you interact online - is your voice clear? If not, take time to redefine it.

☐ ## Audit Your Site & Socials - Tuneup!
Are your fan journeys leading to dead ends? Is your brand consistent across the web?

☐ ## Set Out Your Capture Buckets
If you don't have a system for fan ownership—email list, CTAs, and sanctuary time to catch the rain!

☐ ## Get Your Email List Firing
Become an email marketing student - check open rates, resend emails that resonated, build your list weekly.

☐ ## Initiate Your 5 Touchpoints
DM people who leave comments, start a conversation in your email replies, or send a personal shout out - see what happens (it may lead to a real fan)

The Bond Marketing Action Plan

Create Your Fan Sanctuary
Maybe it's a text messaging list, maybe it's an app that allows VIP access, research what works best for you and build.

Rely On Repeatable Strategies
Test what is working and do those consistently. It's not a fluke it's a *system.*

Introduce A Paid Ad Strategy
Only after you have a repeatable strategy should you pay for ads that drive results (results = touchpoints.)

Get Your Community Interacting
Start two-way conversations and get fans talking not only to you but also to each other.

Focus on Consistent Sales
Be sure to plan sales launches and offers in advance

Don't Forget to Celebrate Your Wins As You Go
Each real bonded fan is a cause for celebration. Don't ever forget this - take the time to acknowledge your journey.

Parting Thought...

Bond Marketing doesn't expire.

Your people are your people.

Real connection is timeless.

It's not at the mercy of algorithm changes, fleeting trends, or industry shifts.

It's about real people, real connections, and real impact.

When you invest in your fans—not just numbers—you build something that lasts.

Your people will stick with you, through every release, reinvention, and life change.
This is how you take control of your career on your terms. Not by chasing attention, but by creating something meaningful that stands the test of time.

When you focus on real fans, you own your music career on *your* terms.

ABOUT
THE
AUTHOR

Ariel Hyatt

Since the dawn of the digital music age, Ariel has helped thousands of artists across all genres and career stages navigate the confusing and ever-changing music business with greater ease and efficiency. Her passion, expertise, and intuitive guidance make her a transformative force for musicians looking to accelerate their careers. Ariel's greatest strengths lie in making what feels overwhelming and complicated seem easy and digestible, teaching, creating artist systems, and her relentless quest for learning.

Ariel's firsthand experience with creative struggles shapes her mission to support artists. Through her work as an author, podcaster, and course creator, she provides tools to help musicians thrive. "Growing a music career has a science to it, but no one-size-fits-all map—each artist's path is their own."

Her commitment to educating artists has taken her to over 70 conferences in 13 countries, including SXSW, CMJ, MONDO, Vivid Sydney, Hubspot Ignite, and Social Media Week New York. She has also toured Canada and Australia, teaching marketing masterclasses to artists and created multiple courses for top music industry colleges and universities.

She has written six books on PR, crowdfunding, and new media, including Music Success in 9 Weeks, Cyber PR for Musicians, Social Media Tuneup, Crowdstart, and The Ultimate Guide to Music Publicity.

Born and raised in New York City, Ariel lives in Manhattan with her husband, son, and 20-year-old tabby, Hunter C. Thompson (the "C" stands for cat). She serves on the Women in Music and Sweet Relief Musicians Fund boards and is a proud graduate of Leadership Music in Nashville. She is the creator of RISE: Resources, Impact, Support & Empowerment - a network of female music industry veterans.

ABOUT
CYBER PR

My agency, Cyber PR, provides musicians and music-related brands with the tools and knowledge they need to succeed in today's music industry. My team and I help our clients take charge of their fan bases.

Our music publicity campaigns have been helping artists expand their reach, reputation, and critical reception for over 25 years.

Years ago, I realized that while publicity is essential, it's just one piece of the puzzle. Most artists I talk to are missing two critical things: a plan and a team. That's why I created Cyber PR—to bridge that gap. The problem is that most teams aren't accessible to artists until they're already well-established, but we believe independent musicians deserve the same strategic support from the start.

Our Total Tuneups provide comprehensive marketing plans that help our clients build a strong and sustainable brand foundation. At the same time, our coaching services guide them through the ever-evolving music business landscape.

Our greatest strengths are making what feels overwhelming and complicated seem digestible, teaching artists systems, and micro coaching them to the next success steps.

We love rolling up our sleeves to help musicians connect to themselves first and then to their fans in meaningful ways.

If you would like to add true thinking partners to your journey, I would love to talk to you.

Find me here:

CyberPRMusic.com

There is a Companion Guide to This Book!
Step 2 of the Bond Marketing Funnel is Completely Outlined in this Guide

Building a bonded fanbase starts with owning your audience—but if your social media presence is weak, inconsistent, or scattered, you're losing opportunities before you even realize it.

From Buzz to Bond teaches you how to create deep, lasting fan relationships, and Social Media Tune Up is your companion guide to ensuring your online presence actually reflects your brand and attracts the right fans.

This book gives you a step-by-step system—the same proven process we use at Cyber PR— to optimize your socials, increase engagement, and drive real traffic to your music.

What You'll Get Inside:
- A complete audit system to assess and improve your social media presence
- Proven platform-specific strategies to fix broken fan journeys
- Checklists to keep your online brand clear and compelling
- Facebook, Instagram, TikTok, LinkedIn, and YouTube included
- Winning website optimization tips as well

Social Media Tune Up walks you through exactly what to do—no fluff, just clear, actionable guidance.

Buy here: **https://bit.ly/SMtuneup**

© Ariel Hyatt. All Rights Reserved 2025

No part of this publication may be reproduced, distributed, or transmitted in any form or by any means, including photocopying, recording, or other electronic or mechanical methods without prior written permission of the publisher, except in the case of brief quotations embodied in critical reviews and certain other noncommercial uses permitted by copyright law.

Limit of Liability / Disclaimer of Warranty: While the intent of the publisher and author is to offer information on music publicity and they have used their best efforts in preparing this book, they make no representations or warranties concerning the accuracy or completeness of the contents of this book and specifically disclaim any implied warranties of merchantability or fitness for a particular purpose. No warranty may be created or extended by sales representatives or written sales materials. The advice and strategies contained herein may not be suitable for your situation, and the publisher and author do not guarantee the attainment of a paying job. You should consult with a professional where appropriate. Neither the publisher nor the author shall be liable for any loss, profit, or other commercial damages, including but not limited to special, incidental, consequential, or other damages.